THOMAS CRANE PUBLIC LIBRARY

QUINCY MASS

CITY APPROPRIATION

THE HUMAN BODY

THE MUSCULAR SYSTEM

By Greg Roza

Gareth Stevens
Publishing

Please visit our website, www.garethstevens.com. For a free color catalog of all our high-quality books, call toll free 1-800-542-2595 or fax 1-877-542-2596.

Library of Congress Cataloging-in-Publication Data

Roza, Greg.
The muscular system / Greg Roza.
p. cm. — (The human body)
Includes index.
ISBN 978-1-4339-6586-9 (pbk.)
ISBN 978-1-4339-6587-6 (6-pack)
ISBN 978-1-4339-6584-5 (library binding)
1. Musculoskeletal system—Juvenile literature. I. Title.
QP301.R7 2011
612.7—dc23

2011023972

First Edition

Published in 2012 by
Gareth Stevens Publishing
111 East 14th Street, Suite 349
New York, NY 10003

Designer: Daniel Hosek
Editor: Greg Roza

Photo credits: Cover, p. 1 Science Faction/Getty Images; all backgrounds, pp. 5, 8, 11 (all images), 13, 17 (digestive system), 21, 23, 25, 28 (all images), 29 Shutterstock.com; pp. 6–7, 15, 17 (peristalsis) MedicalRF.com/Getty Images; p. 7 Innerspace Imaging/Science Photo Library/Getty Images; p. 19 Mike Harrington/Digital Vision/Getty Images; p. 27 MN Chan/Getty Images.

Printed in the United States of America

CPSIA compliance information: Batch #CW12GS: For further information contact Gareth Stevens, New York, New York at 1-800-542-2595.

Contents

Words in the glossary appear in **bold** type the first time they are used in the text.

Move Your Muscles!

Think of all the ways the muscles in your body move in a normal day. Your hand muscles turn doorknobs and hold pens. Your arm muscles lift phones and throw balls. Your leg muscles help you kick, jump, and run. Even the muscles in your face allow you to show emotion. Muscles are very important to the human body. Without them, we wouldn't be able to move!

However, there's much more to our muscles than you might imagine. Some muscles, such as the heart, work without us even thinking about them. Some help us swallow food or go to the bathroom. Let's take a look at the three types of muscles in the human body and find out how they keep us alive and kicking!

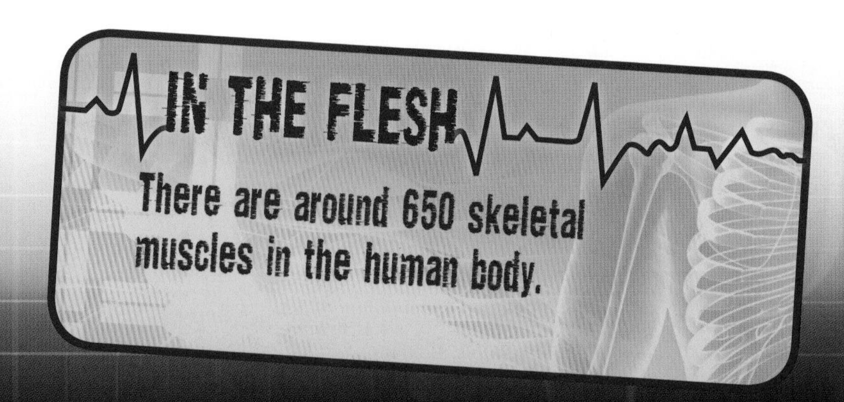

GIANT MUSCLES!

Bodybuilders are people who increase the size of their muscles by lifting weights regularly and eating a special diet. Lifting weights damages the cells of the muscles. However, the muscles grow larger and stronger as they heal, especially with the right diet. **Protein** is a **nutrient** found in many foods that helps repair damaged muscle cells. Bodybuilders use this to their advantage, but so can regular people. We'll learn more about this later.

This person is doing an exercise called a bench press. It helps build strong muscles in the arms and chest.

Skeletal Muscle

Skeletal muscles are the muscles attached to bones. They're complex body parts made up of increasingly smaller bundles of long, **cylindrical** tissues. A single muscle is made up of cylindrical parts called fascicles. The fascicles are bundled together inside a covering called the epimysium. A single fascicle contains numerous muscle cells, which are called fibers. Between all muscle fibers and fascicles are connective tissues that hold the cylindrical tissues in place. Blood vessels and nerves run through the connective tissues.

IN THE FLESH

The Achilles tendon connects the calf muscle to the heel. It's named after Achilles, a hero of Greek mythology. He died when an arrow hit his only weak spot—his heel.

tendon

Similar to the fascicles, muscle fibers contain bundles of cylindrical proteins called myofibrils. Inside the myofibrils are thick and thin **filaments**, also called myofilaments, that can slide past each other. This sliding action is what allows muscles to contract, or grow shorter.

Skeletal muscles are also called striated muscles. This is because they have light and dark striations, or stripes, when viewed under a microscope.

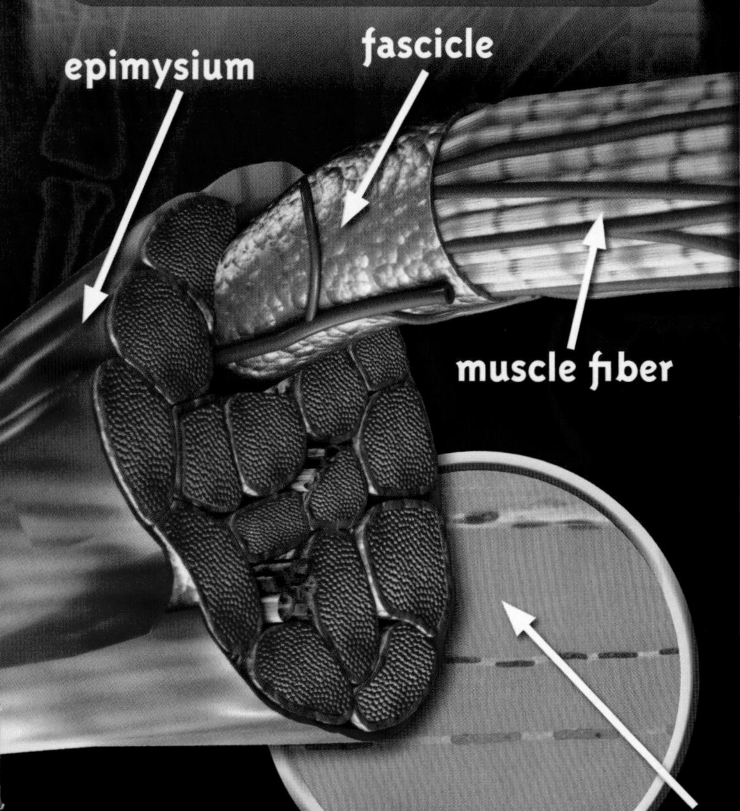

TENDONS

Where muscles meet bones, they taper down to tough yet flexible cords called tendons. Tendons transfer motion from muscles to bones. They grow into the bones to form a strong connection that's very hard to break. The largest tendons in the body are the Achilles tendons. They attach the heels to the back of the calves. They're thick and strong because they're used so often.

Unlike the other two kinds of muscles, skeletal muscles are moved voluntarily. This means we move them just by thinking about it. When you want to move your body, electrical impulses travel from your brain, down your spinal column, through your nerves, and to the cells of your skeletal muscles.

This picture demonstrates how nerve cells communicate with muscle cells.

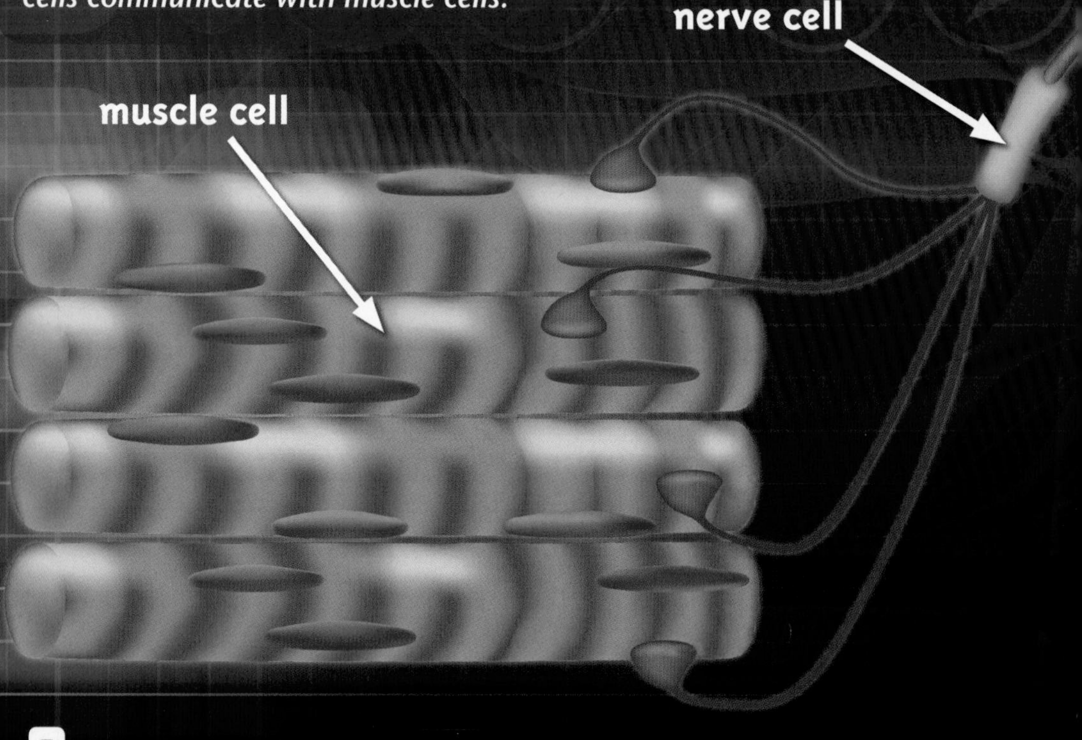

nerve cell

muscle cell

Between the nerve cells and muscle cells is a very tiny gap. The electrical impulses tell the nerve cells to release special chemicals that cross the gap and enter the muscle cells. The chemicals tell the myofilaments inside the muscle cells to slide past each other. The cells—which are normally long and cylindrical—become shorter and fatter. This action tightens the muscle and creates movement, which is transferred along the tendons to the bones.

IN THE FLESH

Tetanus is also the name of an illness caused by a kind of **bacteria**. It causes the muscles to contract uncontrollably.

TWITCH AND TETANUS

Muscle cells are either "off" (relaxed) or "on" (contracted). However, the amount of time the cell remains contracted varies. A quick, single contraction is called a twitch. A twitch occurs, for example, when you blink your eye, which takes a fraction of a second. When a series of twitches occur one after another, the muscle cells remain contracted for a longer period of time. This sustained contraction is called tetanus.

Skeletal muscles come in pairs called extensors and flexors. These muscles create a push/pull effect to allow our body parts to move in two directions. An extensor extends, or straightens, a joint. A flexor flexes, or bends, a joint.

Let's take a look at the muscles of the upper arm. On the back of your arm is an extensor muscle called the triceps. When this muscle contracts, it causes your arm to extend at the elbow and straighten out. Once your arm is extended, the triceps muscle relaxes. A muscle called the biceps is on the front of your arm. This muscle is a flexor. When the biceps muscle contracts, your elbow flexes, or bends. Once your elbow is bent, the biceps relaxes.

IN THE FLESH

The tongue is made up of numerous muscles. Unlike most skeletal muscles, the tongue is attached to bone on one end only.

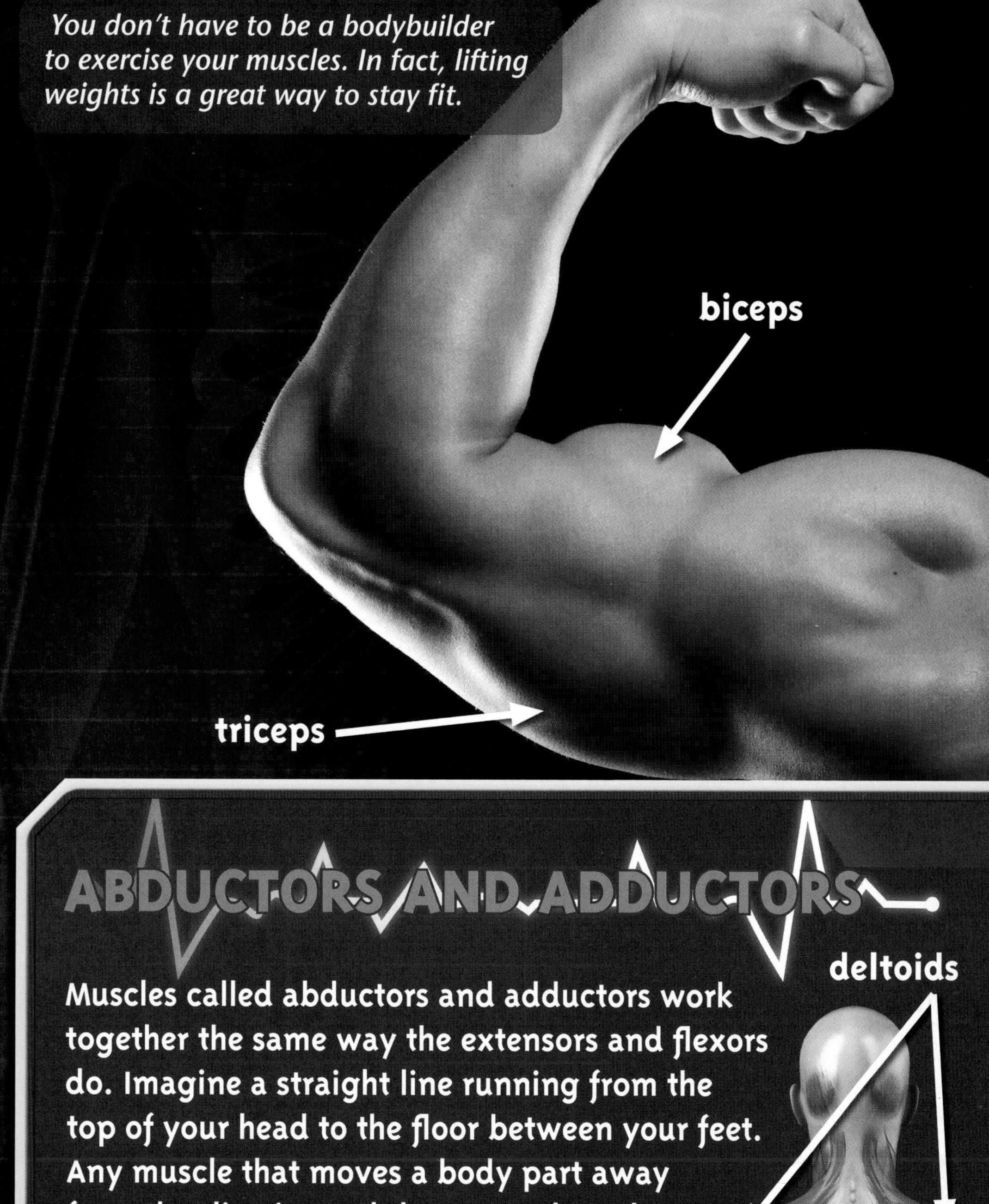

You don't have to be a bodybuilder to exercise your muscles. In fact, lifting weights is a great way to stay fit.

ABDUCTORS AND ADDUCTORS

Muscles called abductors and adductors work together the same way the extensors and flexors do. Imagine a straight line running from the top of your head to the floor between your feet. Any muscle that moves a body part away from that line is an abductor, such as the deltoid muscles of your shoulders. Any muscle that moves a body part toward the line is an adductor, such as the "lats," which are the largest muscles of your back.

deltoids

lats

Cardiac Muscle

The heart is made mostly of cardiac muscle. This kind of muscle makes up the largest layer of the heart walls, known as the myocardium. Cardiac muscle is striated. The actions that cause cardiac muscle cells to contract are nearly the same as those in skeletal muscle cells. However, cardiac muscles are much shorter. They branch out and connect together in a complex network.

Cardiac muscle moves involuntarily. That means we don't have to think about moving our cardiac muscle to keep our heart beating. Individual cardiac muscle cells aren't told to contract by electrical impulses from the brain. The electrical signals are generated within the myocardium itself. Special cardiac cells—called pacemaker cells—use chemical reactions to start the signals, which then travel from cell to cell throughout the heart.

IN THE FLESH

Cardiac muscle can contract and relax more than 2 billion times in a single lifetime!

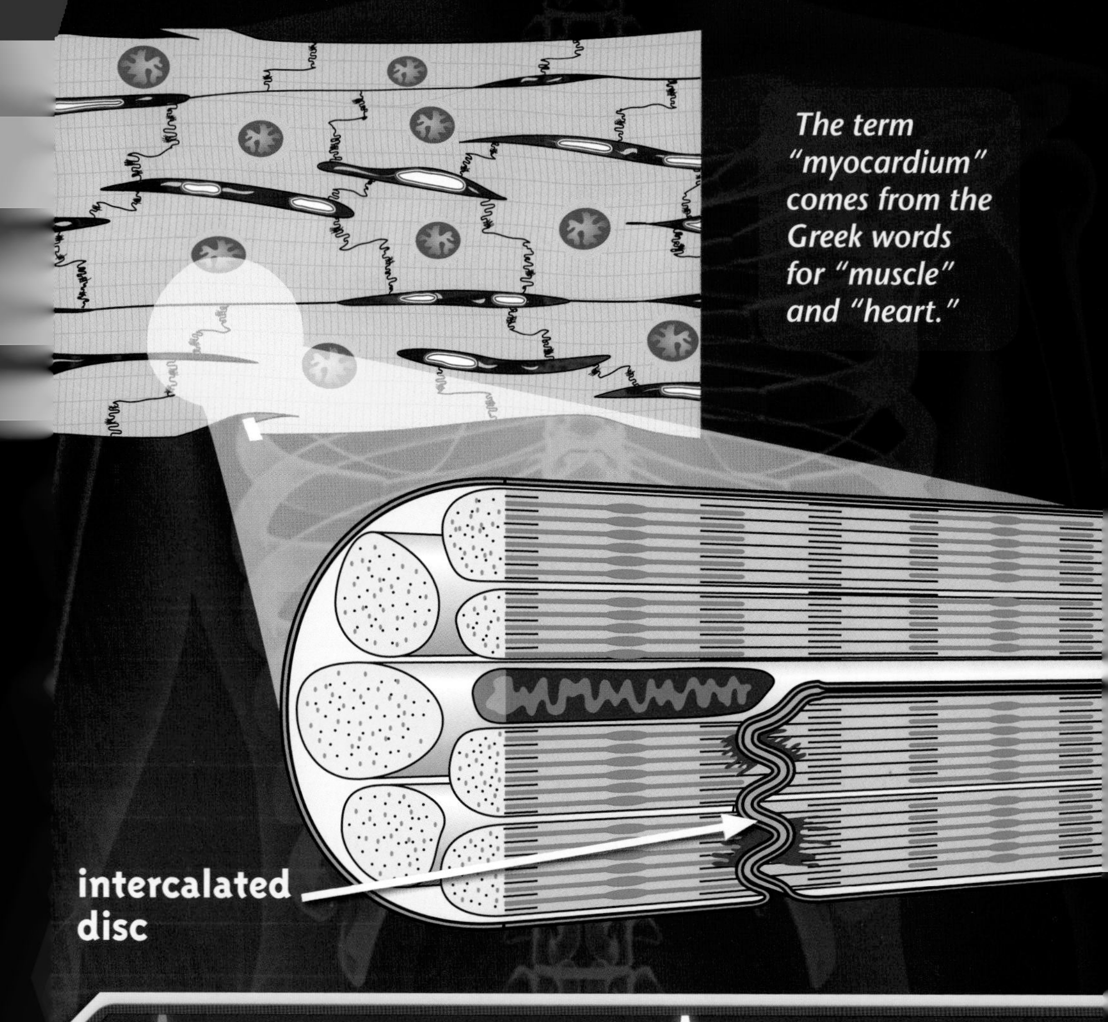

The term "myocardium" comes from the Greek words for "muscle" and "heart."

INTERCALATED DISCS

An intercalated disc is the meeting point between cardiac muscle cells. These **membranes** have two functions. First, they help bind cells to each other. Second, they allow the cells to communicate with each other. Similar to the way nerve cells communicate with skeletal muscle cells, one cardiac muscle cell releases chemicals into an intercalated disc. The next cell receives the chemicals and passes the information along as an electrical impulse.

Smooth Muscle

Smooth muscle is involuntary muscle that forms the inner surfaces of many hollow organs in the body. Smooth muscle cells are much smaller than skeletal muscle cells. They're wide in the middle and tapered on the ends. Many cells fit tightly together to form thin sheets. The sheets lie one on top of another to form thick layers of muscle.

Just like the other two types of muscle, smooth muscle cells contain bundles of thick and thin filaments that move past each other during contraction. However, smooth muscle also has additional filaments that crisscross the cell and hold the bundles together. When a smooth muscle cell contracts, the additional filaments tighten and squeeze the cells together like the drawstring on the opening of a purse or backpack.

IN THE FLESH

When viewed under a microscope, smooth muscle doesn't have striations. This is where its name comes from.

Relaxed smooth muscle cells have a fusiform shape. That means they grow narrow on both ends.

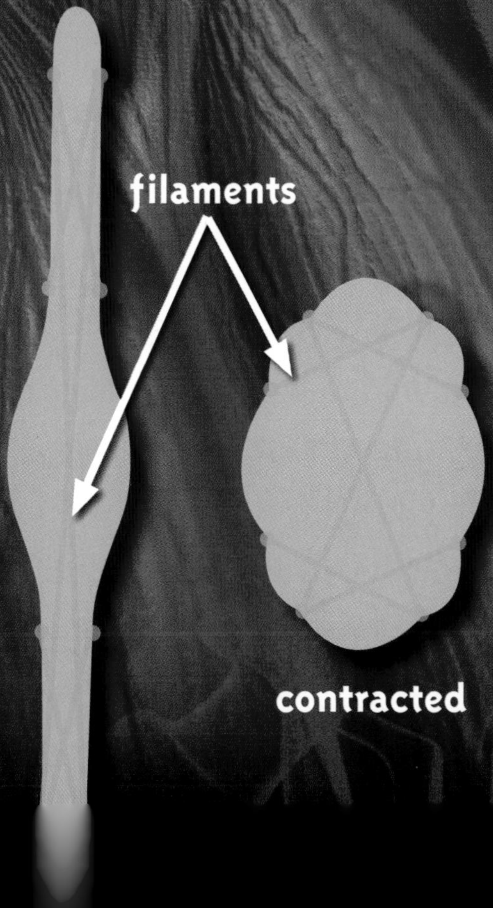

filaments

contracted

GET THE MESSAGE

The manner in which smooth muscle transmits electrical impulses varies. Some smooth muscle reacts to **hormones** in the blood. Some has pacemaker cells to initiate electrical impulses. Smooth muscle cells relay electrical impulses similar to the way cardiac muscle cells do. Chemical messengers pass through the boundary between cells. Although all smooth muscle is involuntary, some receives electrical impulses from the brain by way of the nervous system.

Smooth muscle helps the body carry out numerous functions necessary for life without us even thinking about it. Most helps in the transportation of nutrients, chemicals, and waste products throughout the body. Smooth muscle can even be found in the walls of blood vessels, which are the parts of the circulatory system that transport blood. It helps keep the blood pumping properly.

The digestive system—which includes the esophagus, stomach, and intestines—is lined with smooth muscle. It keeps food and waste products moving. The esophagus has two sets of smooth muscle. One set runs up and down the esophagus, and the other set forms rings around the passage. During a process called peristalsis, these muscles work together to move food down to the stomach.

IN THE FLESH

Smooth muscles in an organ called the urinary **bladder** contract to push liquid waste, or urine, from the body when we go to the bathroom.

MULTIUNIT SMOOTH MUSCLE

There are two kinds of smooth muscle. Single-unit smooth muscle is the tightly packed form discussed so far. Multiunit smooth muscle, the less common form, is made up of cells that act independently of each other. Each cell connects to a nerve cell so the body can tell it how to act in different situations. Multiunit smooth muscle can be found in the eye. It causes the iris to grow larger or smaller to let in more or less light.

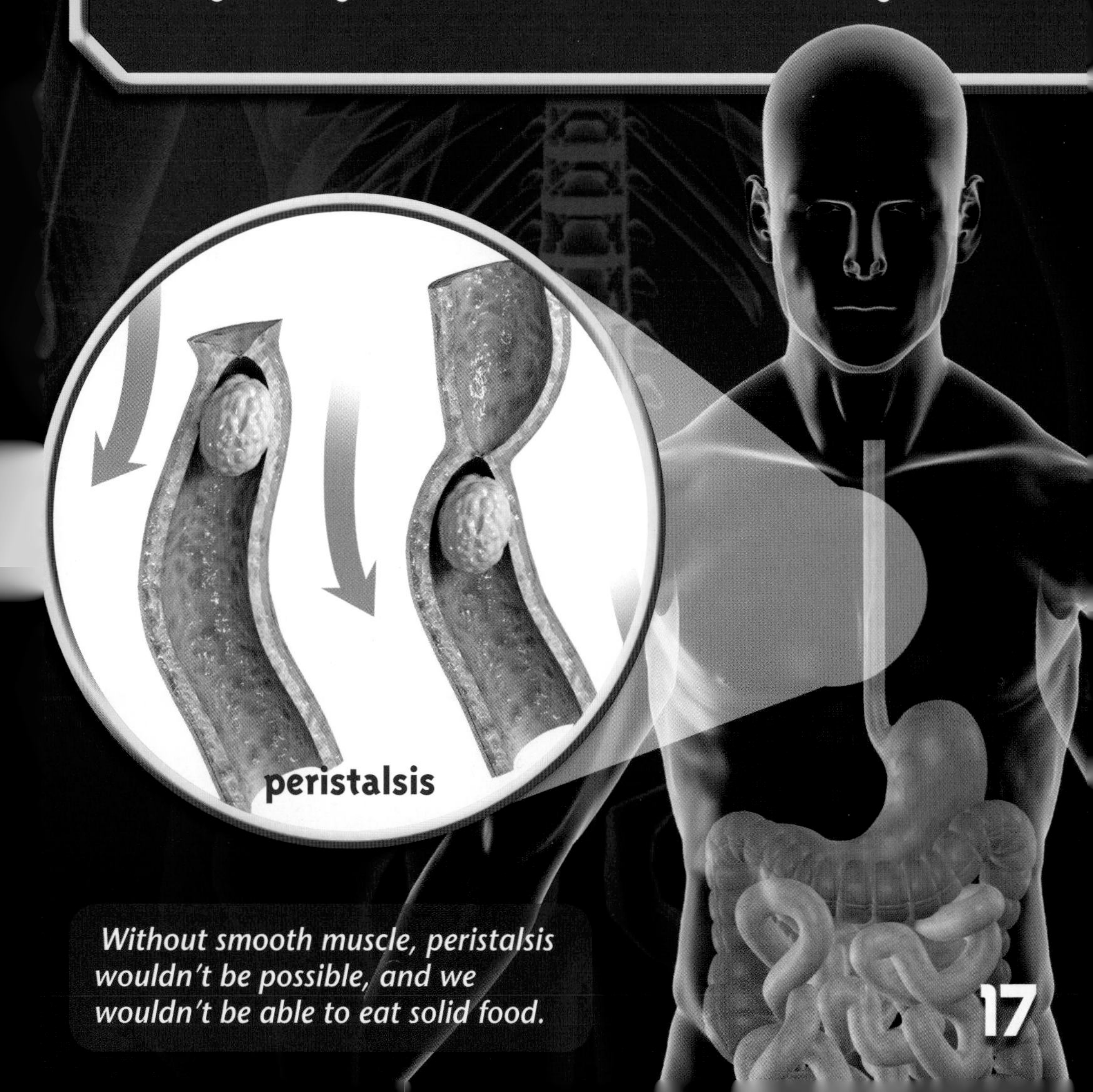

Without smooth muscle, peristalsis wouldn't be possible, and we wouldn't be able to eat solid food.

Hit the Gym!

Just about every activity you can think of requires the use of muscles—even eating and watching television! However, when we work out at the gym, play a sport, or just take a walk, we're using our muscles to make our whole body healthier. We lose fat, gain muscle, and even prevent illness.

During exercise, the body changes the way it functions to help the muscles work. The lungs take in more oxygen, and the heart rate increases to get more blood to the muscles. This is important because the muscles need oxygen to break down a substance called **glucose**. We get glucose from the foods we eat. Breaking down glucose creates adenosine triphosphate (ATP), which stores the energy that our muscles need to work.

IN THE FLESH

When the body doesn't have enough glucose, it breaks down fat to create ATP. This is why regular, sustained exercise helps keep people trim and healthy.

You should exercise in several different ways to target diffferent muscles. It's a more fun way to stay fit, too!

LIFE FUEL

ATP is present in every cell of the body. It fuels our muscles, but it also provides the rest of our body with the energy necessary to keep us alive. It fuels the activity inside all the cells of the body. ATP also transports substances across membranes in the body. It helps nutrients get where they need to go. The process of combining oxygen with glucose to make ATP is called cellular respiration.

Like car engines, active muscles burn fuel to create power and movement. The muscles contain enough ATP for quick bursts of activity. Then they need to make more. Luckily, the muscles have more than one method of doing this. Burning ATP creates the waste products carbon dioxide and water. It also releases a lot of heat, which is why we get hot and sweaty during a workout.

During sustained exercise—such as running, swimming, and biking—we breathe deeper and faster, and our heart pumps faster to make sure our muscles have enough oxygen to keep on creating ATP. This type of muscle activity is called aerobic exercise. "Aerobic" means "with oxygen." Athletes who require superior **endurance**—such as marathon runners—participate in daily aerobic workouts.

IN THE FLESH

Marathon runners aren't the only people who use cardio exercises to perform at their best. Cyclists, kickboxers, swimmers, mountain climbers, and dancers do, too!

CARDIO WORKOUT

Aerobic exercises are often called "cardio." This is short for "cardiovascular system." The cardiovascular system transports oxygen to the muscles and the rest of the body. The main parts of this system are the heart, blood vessels, and blood. However, it also includes the lungs. Regular aerobic exercise strengthens the cardiovascular system and makes it more efficient. It keeps blood pressure at a healthy level, burns calories, improves physical endurance, and builds strong muscles.

A marathon is a 26.2-mile (42.2 km) race. Participants must be in excellent shape to compete.

Sometimes the muscles don't have enough oxygen to continue breaking down glucose. When muscles run out of oxygen, the glucose instead breaks down into carbon dioxide and a chemical called lactic acid. Lactic acid is what makes our muscles sore during and after exercise. However, muscles also use it as fuel to continue working. This type of muscle activity is called anaerobic exercise. "Anaerobic" means "without oxygen."

Anaerobic muscle activity happens during exercises that last from 30 seconds to 2 minutes. After that, muscles begin to get enough oxygen for aerobic activity. Strength training is a form of anaerobic exercise. When lifting weights, our muscles use quick bursts of energy that don't need to be sustained. This activity creates lactic acid, which makes the muscles sore.

IN THE FLESH

Not using muscles enough can result in muscle atrophy, which is a wasting away or loss of muscle tissue.

You don't have to lift heavy weights to benefit from strength training. The more you do it, however, the easier it will be to lift heavier weights.

WHY IS STRENGTH TRAINING GOOD FOR ME?

Anaerobic exercise results in the buildup of lactic acid in the muscles. This leads first to muscle fatigue, or tiredness, and then **muscle failure**. Muscle fibers actually tear during this process. A period of rest is needed for muscle fibers to repair themselves. Your muscles ache while this is happening, but they also grow larger and stronger. Strength training also burns calories and helps reduce the risk of injuries during physical activities.

Muscle Injuries

Most muscle injuries occur during physical activity or because of overuse. However, they can also occur because of inactivity and illnesses.

A strain, or pulled muscle, is a common muscle injury. Normally, muscle fiber is tightly woven. In a strain, the fibers become overstretched or torn. The muscle usually repairs itself within a week. Some strains, however, can last a long time when not properly cared for. A rupture is a more serious strain. This happens when the muscle is completely torn. A small tear can heal on its own. However, a complete muscle tear requires surgery to fix.

A hematoma is a deep bruise. After a fall or a hard blow to a muscle, blood vessels can break. This causes swelling and a blood clot in the muscle.

IN THE FLESH

A cramp is an involuntary contraction of a muscle that won't relax. Cramps have many causes, including muscle fatigue, injuries, inactivity, and a lack of vitamins and nutrients.

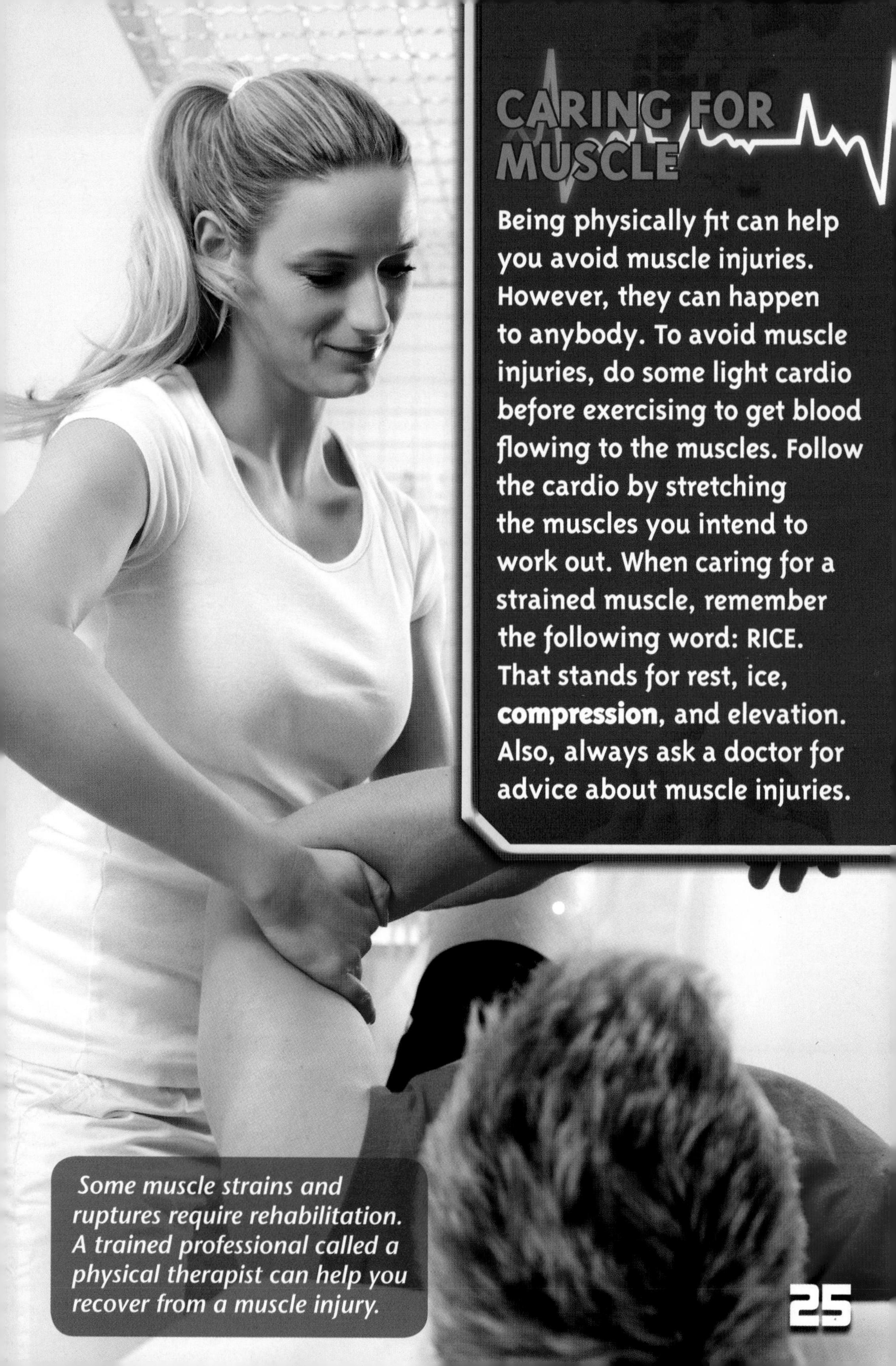

CARING FOR MUSCLE

Being physically fit can help you avoid muscle injuries. However, they can happen to anybody. To avoid muscle injuries, do some light cardio before exercising to get blood flowing to the muscles. Follow the cardio by stretching the muscles you intend to work out. When caring for a strained muscle, remember the following word: RICE. That stands for rest, ice, **compression**, and elevation. Also, always ask a doctor for advice about muscle injuries.

Some muscle strains and ruptures require rehabilitation. A trained professional called a physical therapist can help you recover from a muscle injury.

Muscle Diseases

Diseases of the muscles are called myopathies. Many are caused by the breakdown of muscle fibers. Depending on the specific illness, symptoms may include pain, weakness, cramps, stiffness, bruising, and swelling. Some myopathies are **hereditary**, while others can happen to anybody. Some muscle disorders are the result of other illnesses. They range from mild to severe.

Some of the most life-threatening myopathies are more than 30 hereditary illnesses called muscular dystrophies (MD). These diseases are marked by weakness and death of skeletal muscles. Some forms affect the cardiac muscles. MD can be mild and progress slowly. However, some kinds are severe and fast acting. There's no cure for MD yet, but some people benefit greatly from various forms of treatment.

IN THE FLESH

Neuromuscular diseases are illnesses that affect the nerves that control skeletal muscles. They include Parkinson's disease and multiple sclerosis.

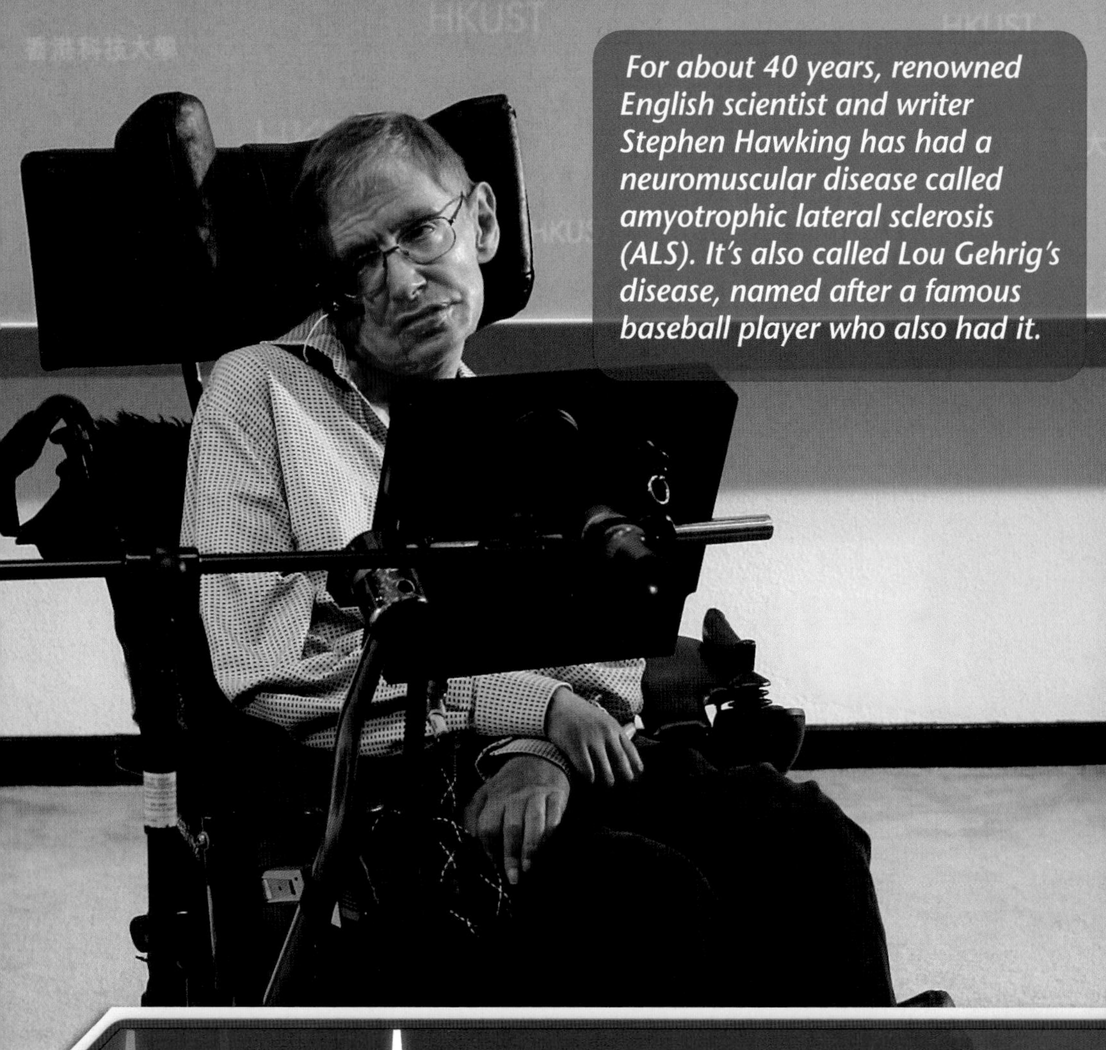

For about 40 years, renowned English scientist and writer Stephen Hawking has had a neuromuscular disease called amyotrophic lateral sclerosis (ALS). It's also called Lou Gehrig's disease, named after a famous baseball player who also had it.

MYOCARDITIS

Myocarditis is a swelling of the myocardium. Most often this occurs as a result of a viral infection. Signs of myocarditis include chest pain, abnormal heartbeat, difficulty breathing, fever, swelling in the ankles and feet, and fatigue. This illness is treated with rest and heart medicines. More serious cases may require surgical procedures. If left untreated, myocarditis can result in heart failure, heart attack, stroke, and sudden death.

Feed Your Muscles

A regular fitness routine is a great way to keep your muscles healthy. However, the harder you work out, the more you need to eat to replace nutrients your muscles use. Healthy **carbohydrates**—such as whole grains, vegetables, and fruits—provide plenty of glucose for our muscles to turn into ATP fuel. Our muscles are made of protein. So, it's important to eat plenty of healthy sources of protein—such as fish, chicken, beans, and nuts—to help our muscles heal and grow stronger. Be sure to drink plenty of water to replace the fluids you lose while working out and avoid muscle cramps.

Our muscular system is the engine that keeps us running. By eating right and getting regular exercise, your muscles are sure to give you the ride of your life!

FACTS ABOUT
The Muscular System

- Muscle is heavier than fat. You could lose fat, gain muscle, and still weigh the same. However, you would be healthier.
- There are 43 facial muscles.
- On average, muscles make up 40 percent of a person's body weight.
- Smooth muscles in a pregnant woman's body help her give birth when the baby is ready to be born.
- Some athletes use drugs called anabolic steroids to build muscles faster. However, these drugs have bad effects on the body.
- Tendonitis is a painful swelling of the tendons. It's usually caused when someone repeats a movement over and over. Tennis players sometimes get tendonitis in their elbows, or "tennis elbow."
- The gap between nerve cells and other cells is called a synapse. The synapse between a nerve cell and a muscle cell is called a neuromuscular junction.

Glossary

bacteria: tiny creatures that can only be seen with a microscope

bladder: an expandable organ that stores liquid waste until it can be removed from the body

carbohydrate: a nutrient in many types of food that the body uses as a source of energy

compression: the act of pressing or squeezing together

cylindrical: shaped like a cylinder or tube

endurance: the ability to do something for a long time without getting tired

filament: a slender strand of a material

glucose: a sugar the body uses for energy

hereditary: passed from parent to child

hormone: a chemical made in the body that tells another part of the body how to function

membrane: a thin tissue in the body

muscle failure: the inability to move a muscle when too much lactic acid builds up in it

nutrient: something a living thing needs to grow and stay alive

protein: a nutrient in many types of food that the body uses to grow, repair tissues, and stay healthy

For More Information

BOOKS

Burstein, John. *The Mighty Muscular and Skeletal Systems: How Do My Bones and Muscles Work?* New York, NY: Crabtree Publishing, 2009.

Parker, Steve. *Muscular and Skeletal Systems.* Mankato, MN: New Forest Press, 2010.

Walker, Richard. *Eyewitness: Human Body*. New York, NY: DK Publishing, 2009.

WEBSITES

Muscular System
yucky.discovery.com/flash/body/pg000123.html
Learn more about skeletal muscles.

Strength Training
kidshealth.org/teen/food_fitness/exercise/strength_training.html
Read more about the benefits of strength training, as well as the right way to get started.

Your Muscles
kidshealth.org/kid/htbw/muscles.html
Read more about the muscular system and see diagrams of muscles.

Index